Pebble® Plus

BURROWING OWLS

by Melissa Hill

Consulting Editor:

Gail Saunders-Smith, PhD

Content Consultant:

Jessica Ehrgott
Bird and Mammal Trainer,
Downtown Aquarium, Denver

CAPSTONE PRESS
a capstone imprint

Pebble Plus is published by Capstone Press,
1710 Roe Crest Drive, North Mankato, Minnesota 56003
www.capstonepub.com

Library of Congress Cataloging-in-Publication Data
Hill, Melissa, 1975– author.
Burrowing Owls / by Melissa Hill.
pages cm.—(Pebble Plus. Owls)
Summary: "Simple text and full-color photographs describe
burrowing owls"—Provided by publisher.
Audience: Ages 5–8.
Audience: K to grade 3.
Includes bibliographical references and index.
ISBN 978-1-4914-6046-7 (library binding)
ISBN 978-1-4914-6052-8 (paperback)
ISBN 978-1-4914-6066-5 (eBook pdf)
1. Burrowing owl—Juvenile literature. I. Title.
QL696.S83H53 2015
598.9'7—dc23   2015005325

Editorial Credits
Jeni Wittrock, editor; Juliette Peters, designer; Morgan Walters, media researcher;
Katy LaVigne, production specialist

Photo Credits
Dreamstime: John Abramo, 15, Rinus Baak, (owl) bottom left 3; Getty Images: J & C Sohns,
7; iStockphoto: bobloblaw, 19, Devonyu, 5, scooperdigital, 17, SteveByland, 22; Shutterstock:
Artography, 3, David Osborn, inset 1, Dean Pennala, (tall grass) back cover, 1, 2, 23, 24, Eric
Isselee, (parakeet) bottom right 6, Feng Yu, (dirt texture) cover and throughout, Feng Yu, 13,
J. Helgason, (tree stump) back cover, 2, 24, Mircea BEZERGHEANU, (rock texture) cover and
throughout, Nick Biemans, 9, Peter Schwarz, cover, Sarah Jessup, 11, Stawek, (map) 10, Tania
Thomson, (owl) back cover, bottom left 6, Tania Thomson, 21

Note to Parents and Teachers

The Owls set supports national curriculum standards for science related to life
science. This book describes and illustrates burrowing owls. The images support
early readers in understanding the text. The repetition of words and phrases
helps early readers learn new words. This book also introduces early readers to
subject-specific vocabulary words, which are defined in the Glossary section. Early
readers may need assistance to read some words and to use the Table of Contents,
Glossary, Read More, Internet Sites, Critical Thinking Using the Common Core,
and Index sections of the book.

Printed in China by Nordica
0415/CA21500542
042015   008837NORDF15

Table of Contents

No Tree for Me

From a hole in the ground,

four yellow eyes peek out.

Most owls live in trees.

But burrowing owls make

homes underground.

Burrowing Owl Bodies

Burrowing owls are 9 inches (23 centimeters) tall. They bob up and down on their long legs. Their big eyes see all around.

Size Comparison

burrowing owl
length:
10 inches
(25 centimeters)

parakeet
length:
6–8 inches
(15–20 centimeters)

The owls watch for predators.
Foxes, coyotes, and hawks
eat burrowing owls.
Brown and tan feathers
make the owls hard to spot.

Underground Owl

Burrowing owls are found in North and South America. They live in deserts, prairies, and other flat, open lands.

Burrowing Owl Range Map

North America

Europe

Asia

Africa

South America

Australia

where burrowing owls live

Animals like prairie dogs dig underground homes. When the prairie dogs move out, burrowing owls move in! The burrows keep owls safe.

On the Hunt

Burrowing owls are hunters. They hunt for beetles, crickets, and other bugs. They also eat tiny rodents, reptiles, and birds.

Burrowing owls fly to
catch bugs in their beaks.
They also grab prey off
the ground with their feet.

Lots of Owls

In spring females lay
up to 12 white eggs. In a
month the fluffy chicks hatch.
The owls live about 8 years.

Some burrowing owls live in large groups. If you're lucky, you may see 100 owls together!

GLOSSARY

burrow—a tunnel in the ground made by an animal

chick—a young owl

desert—an area of land that gets very little rain

hatch—to break out of an egg

prairie—a flat, grassy area with few trees

predator—an animal that hunts other animals for food

prey—an animal that is hunted by other animals for food

reptile—one of a group of animals with scales including snakes and lizards

rodent—one of a group of small mammals with large front teeth for chewing

READ MORE

Marsh, Laura. *Owls.* National Geographic Kids. Washington, D.C.: National Geographic, 2014.

Phillips, Dee. *Burrowing Owl's Hideaway.* The Hole Truth!: Underground Animal Life Series. New York: Bearport, 2015.

Rustad, Martha E. H. *Owls.* Nocturnal Animals. Minneapolis: Jump!, 2014.

INTERNET SITES

FactHound offers a safe, fun way to find Internet sites related to this book. All of the sites on FactHound have been researched by our staff.

Here's all you do:

Visit *www.facthound.com*

Type in this code: 9781491460467

 Check out projects, games and lots more at **www.capstonekids.com**

CRITICAL THINKING USING THE COMMON CORE

1. Most owls live in trees. Why do you think burrowing owls live underground instead? (Integrating Knowledge and Ideas)

2. Groups of burrowing owls live in homes beneath dry, flat land. Can you think of any other animals that live that way? (Integrating Knowledge and Ideas)

INDEX

Word Count: 185
Grade: 1
Early-Intervention Level: 15